1st Recital Series

PIANO ACCOMPANIMENT FOR FLUTE

Including works of:
- James Curnow
- Craig Alan
- Douglas Court
- Mike Hannickel
- Timothy Johnson
- Ann Lindsay

Solos for Beginning
through Early Intermediate
level musicians

CURNOW® MUSIC

EXCLUSIVELY DISTRIBUTED BY

HAL•LEONARD® CORPORATION

7777 W. BLUEMOUND RD. P.O. BOX 13819 MILWAUKEE, WI 53213

Edition Number: CMP 0750.02

1st Recital Series
Solos for Beginning through Early Intermediate level musicians
Piano Accompaniment for Flute

ISBN: 90-431-1683-1

Foreword

High quality solo/recital literature that is appropriate for performers playing at the Beginner through Early Intermediate skill levels is finally here! Each of the **1st RECITAL SERIES** books is loaded with exciting and varied solo pieces that have been masterfully composed or arranged for your instrument.

Included with the solo book there is a professionally recorded CD that demonstrates each piece. Use these examples to help develop proper performance practices. There is also a recording of the accompaniment alone that can be used for performance (and rehearsal) when a live accompanist is not available. A separate solo Flute book is available [edition nr. CMP 0684.02].

Table of Contents

Ludwig van Beethoven
1. ODE TO JOY

Arr. **Timothy Johnson** (ASCAP)

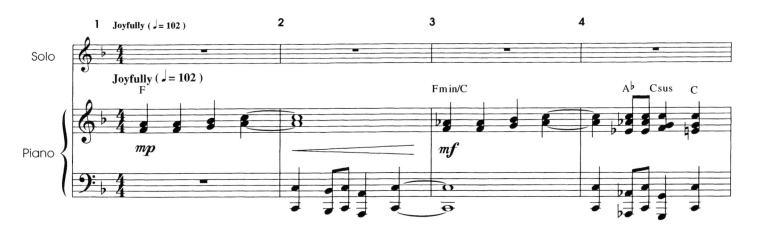

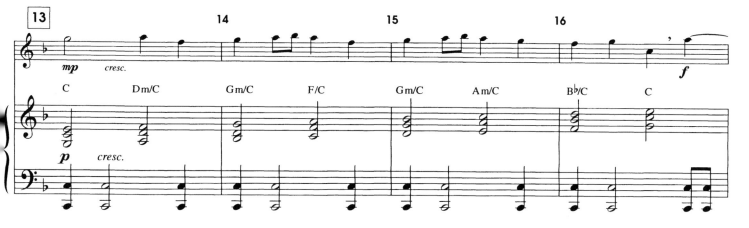

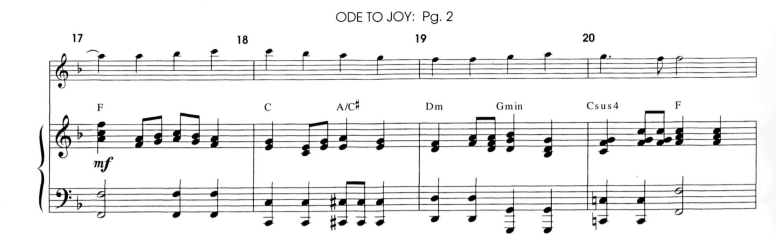

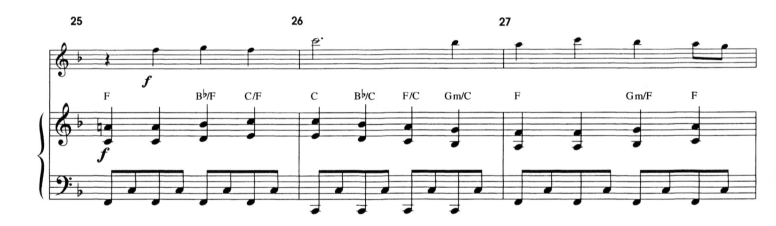

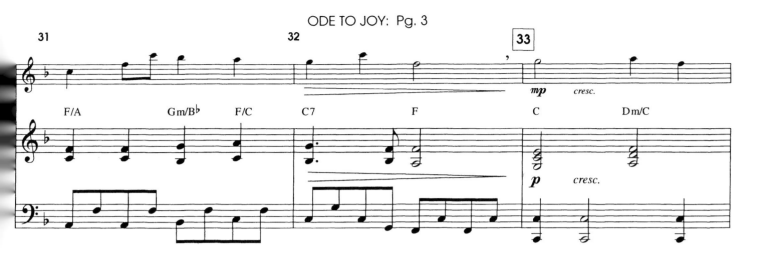

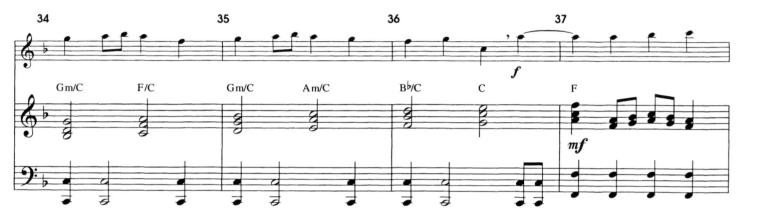

Franz Schubert
2. SANCTUS

Arr. **James Curnow** (ASCAP)

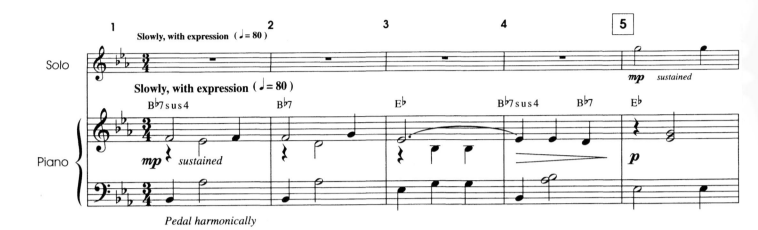

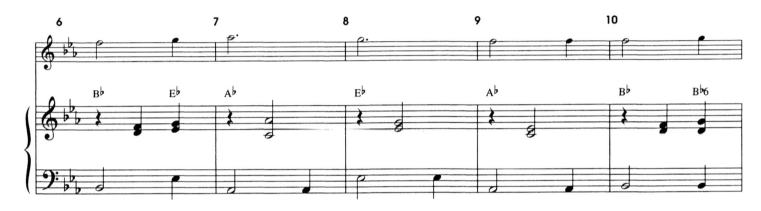

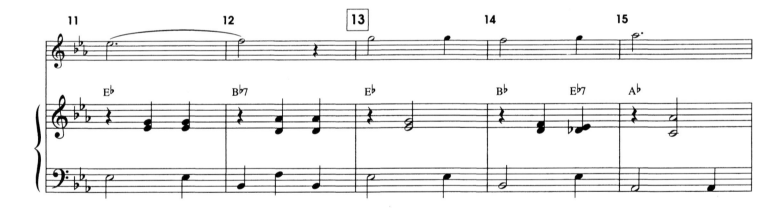

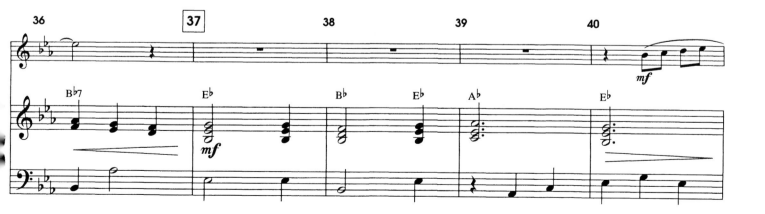

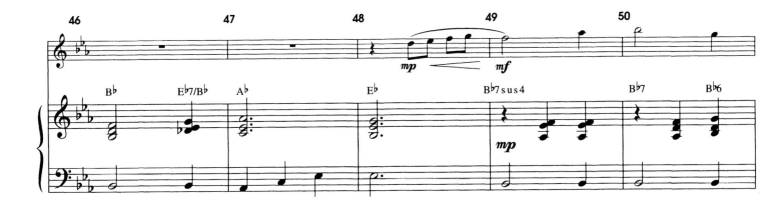

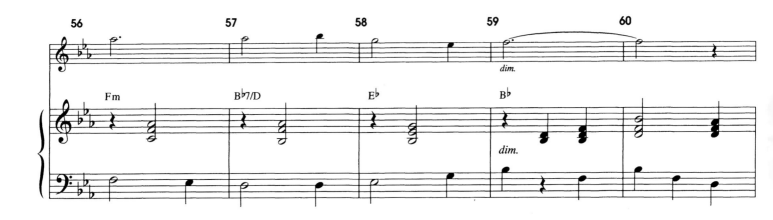

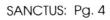

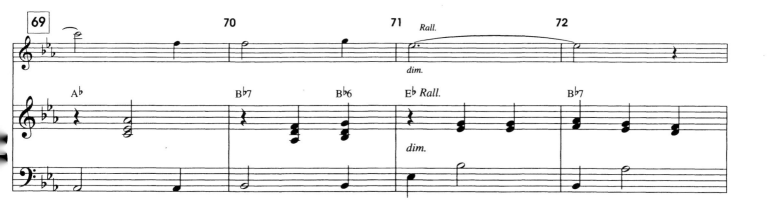

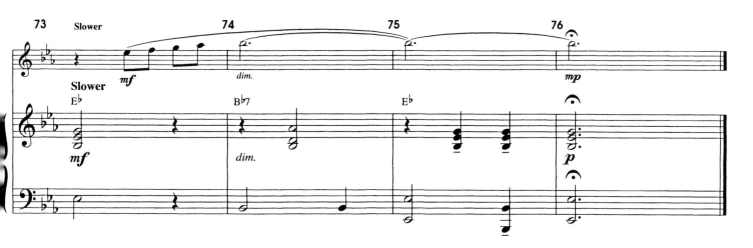

FLUTE

3. MARCH MAJESTIC

Douglas Court (ASCAP)

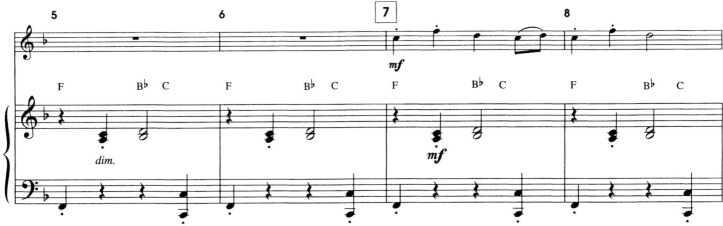

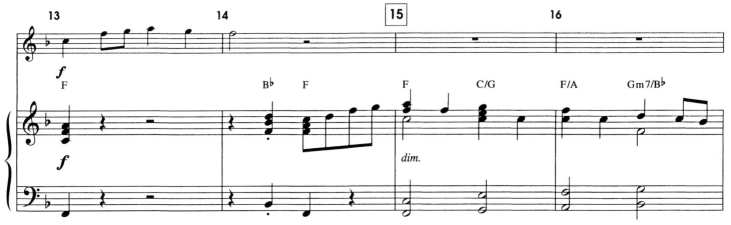

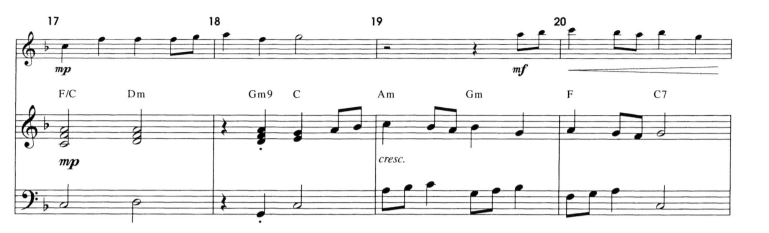

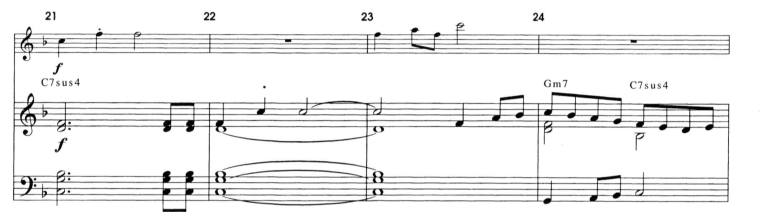

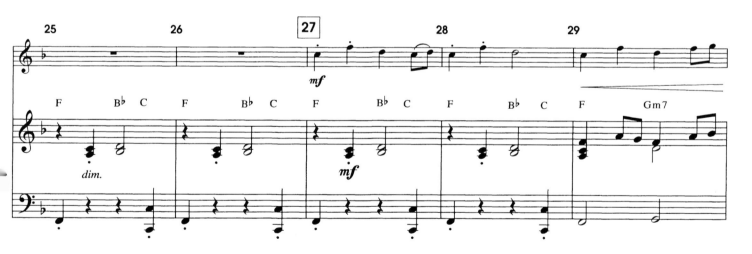

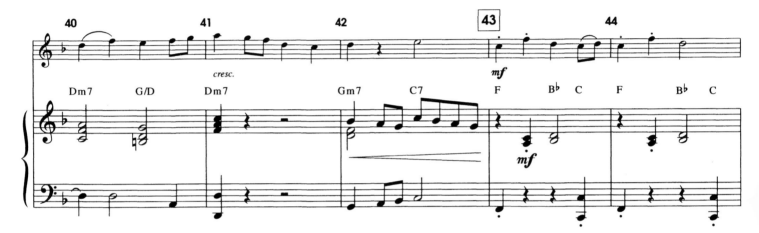

4. THE RED BALLOON

James Curnow (ASCAP)

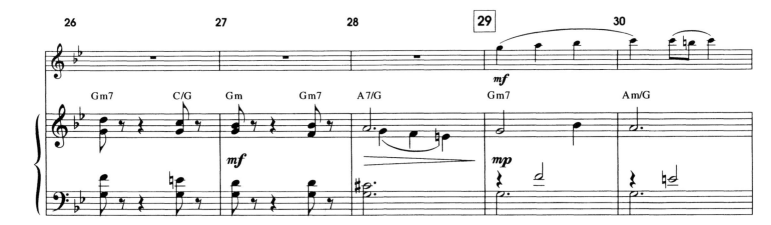

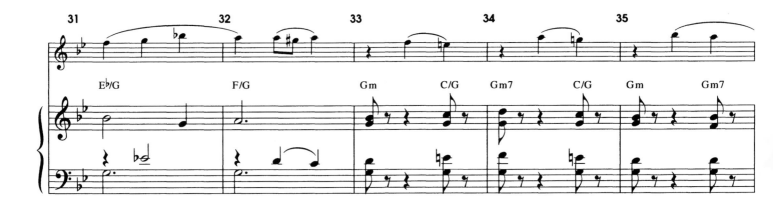

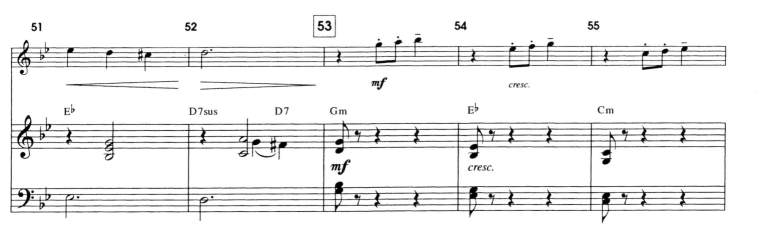

5. RONDO

Timothy Johnson (ASCAP)

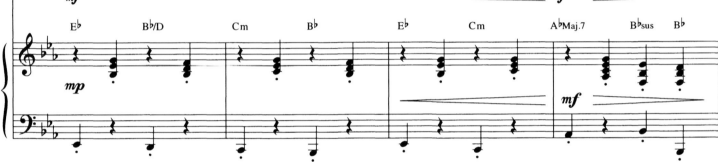

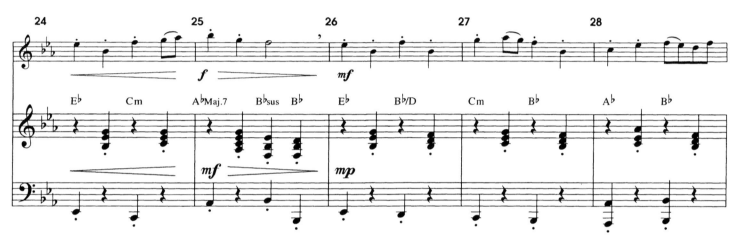

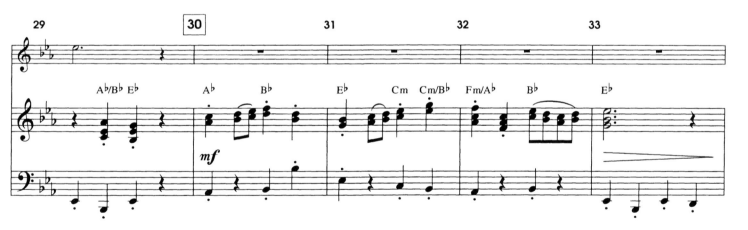

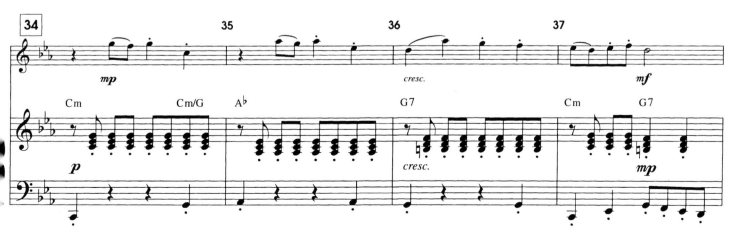

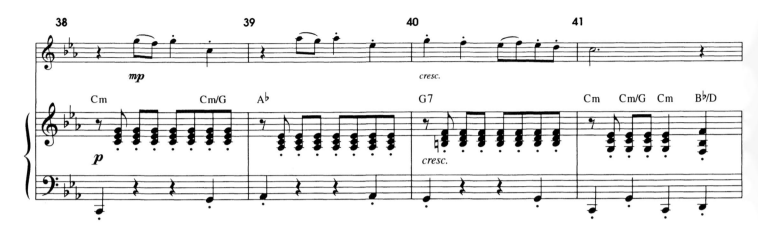

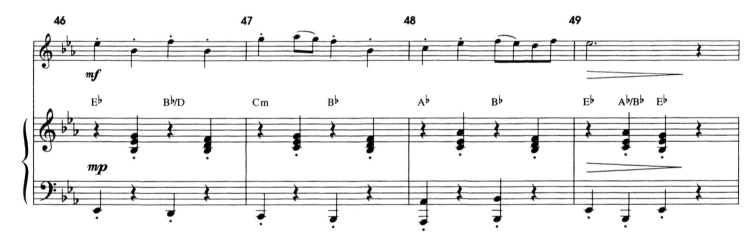

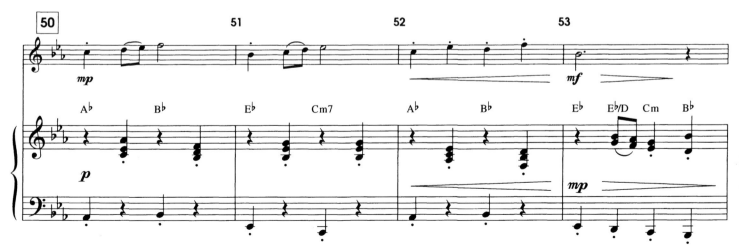

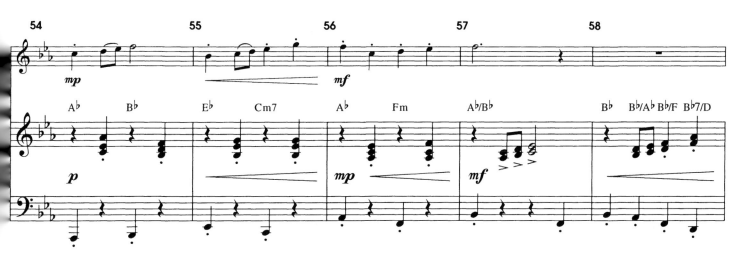

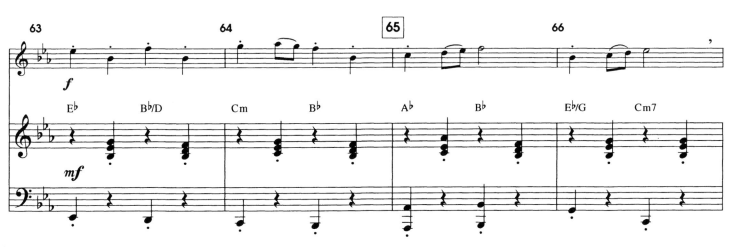

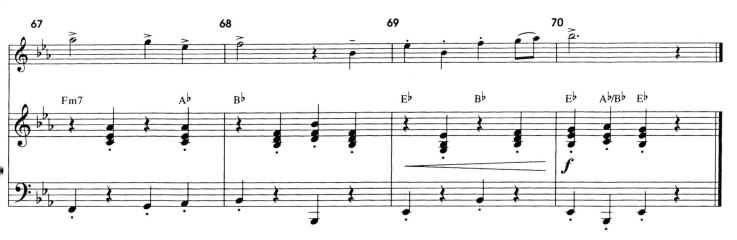

6. THE BUTTERFLY'S ESCAPADE

Mike Hannickel (ASCAP)

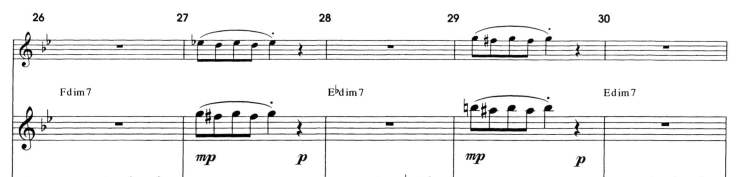

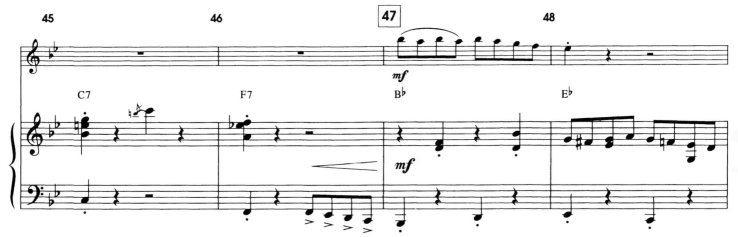

7. SERENADE

Craig Alan (ASCAP)

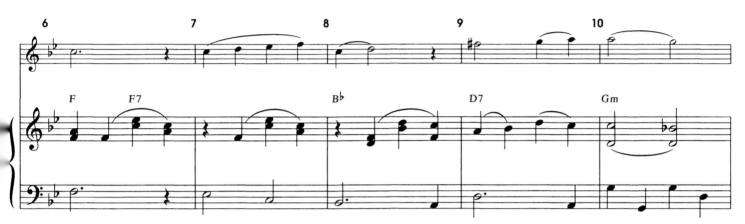

25

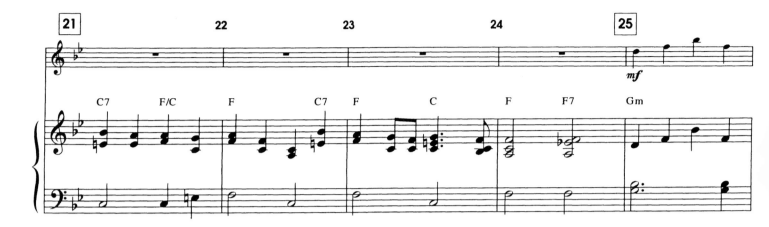

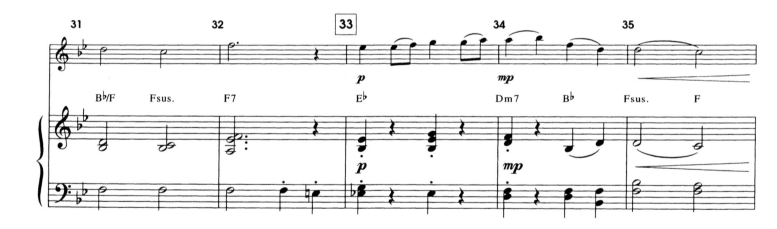

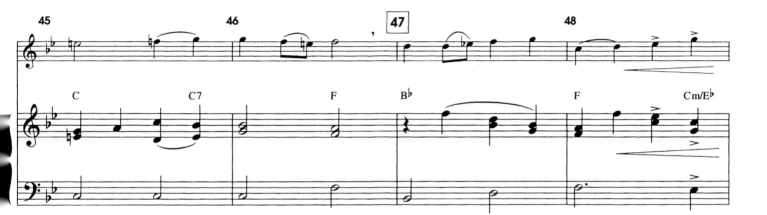

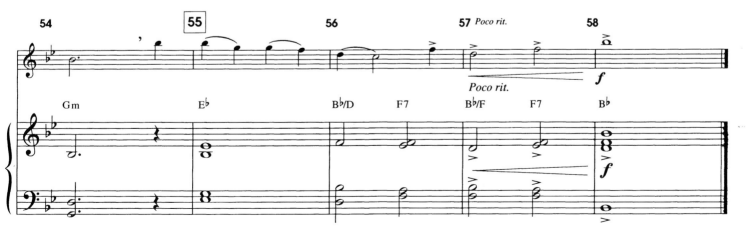

FLUTE

8. FLUTATIONS

Mike Hannickel (ASCAP)

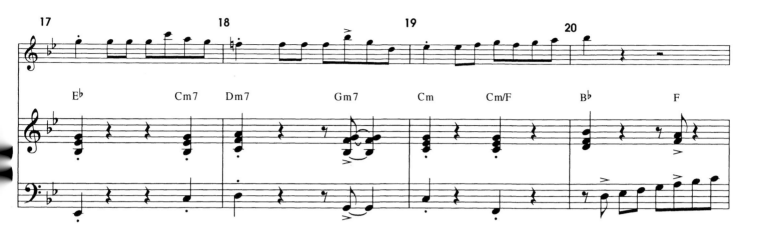

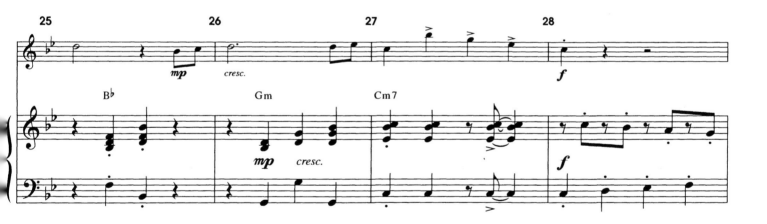

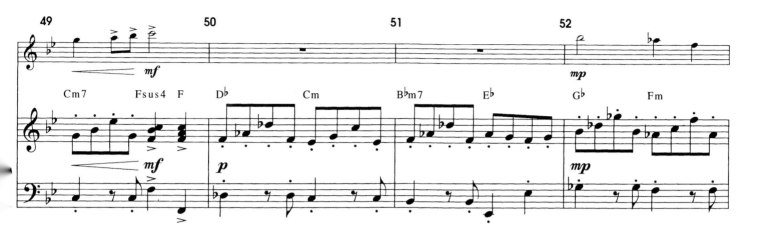

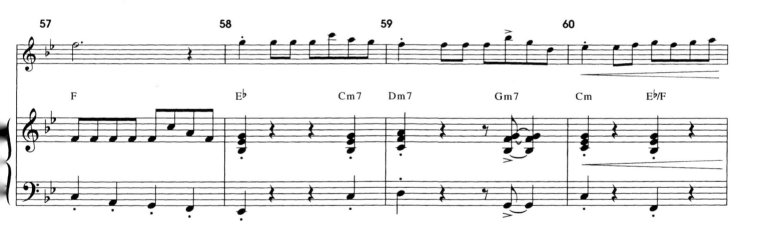

FLUTE

Erik Satie
9. GYMNOPÉDIE No.1
Arr. **Ann Lindsay** (ASCAP)

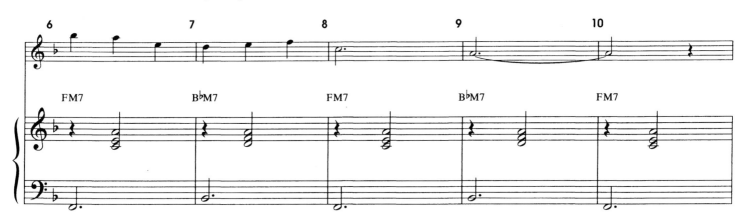

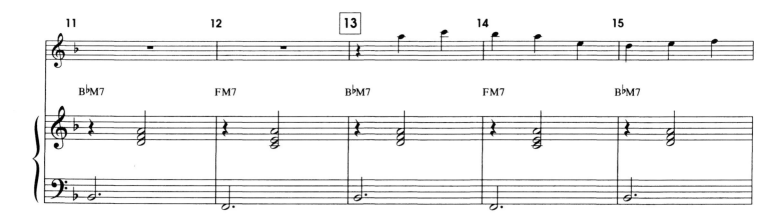

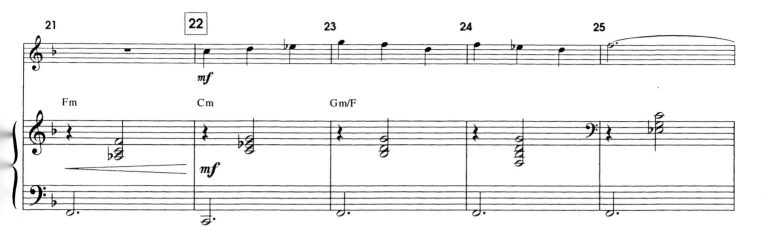

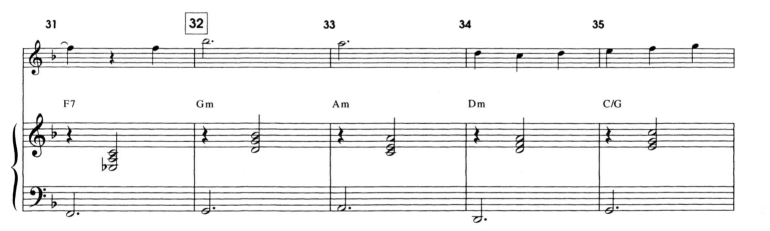

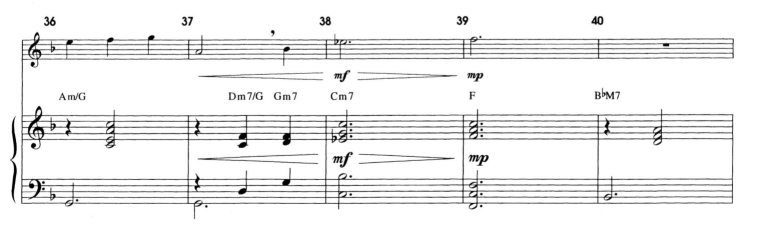

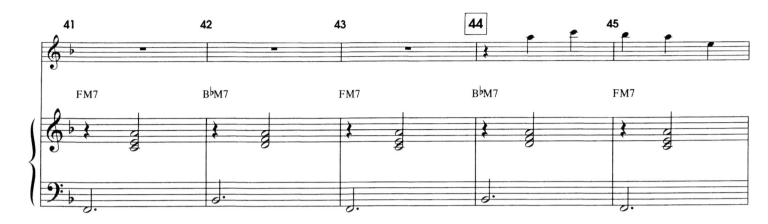

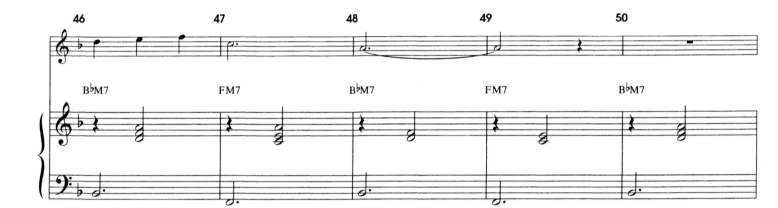

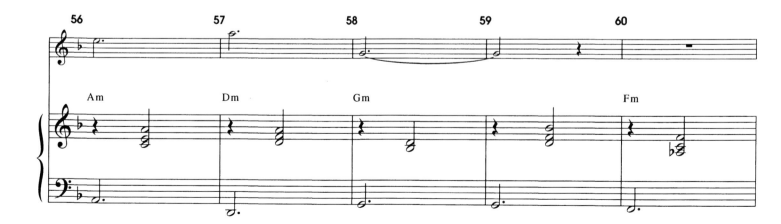

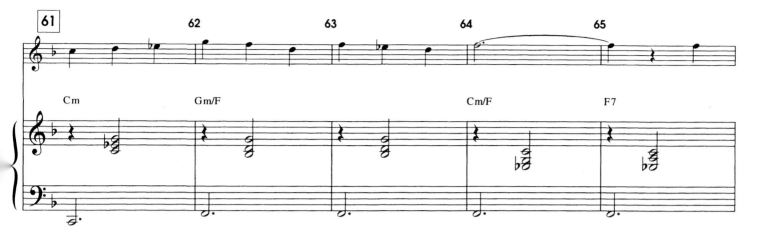

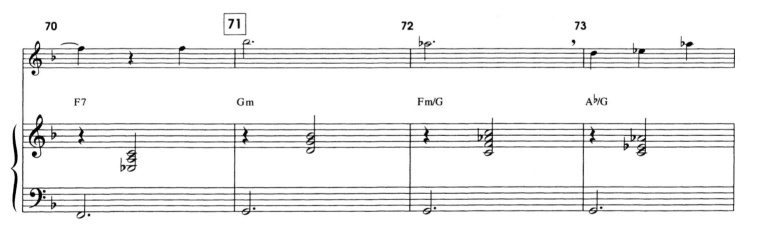

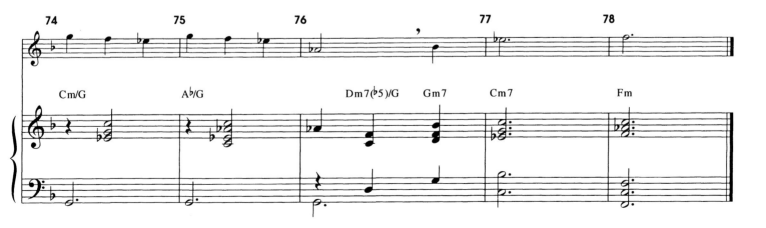

FLUTE

For Debra Scheuerman

10. OH, WHY LEFT I MY HAME?

Scottish Air

Adapted by Mike Hannickel (ASCAP)
After an arrangement by Helen Hopekirk

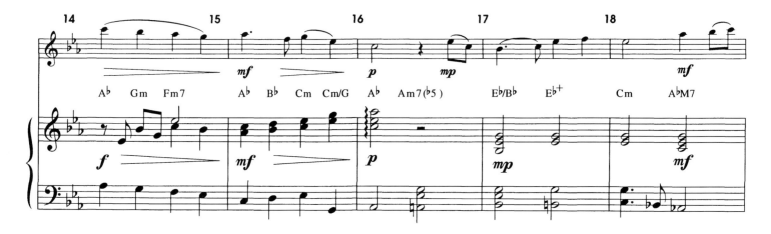

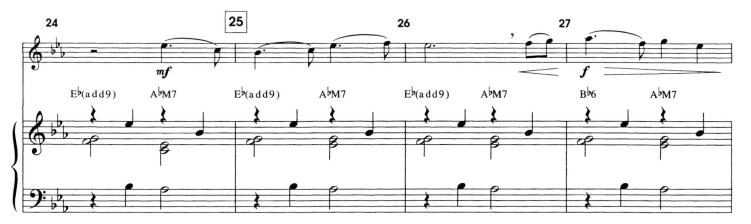

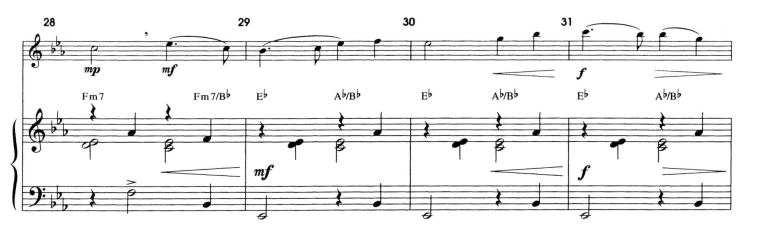

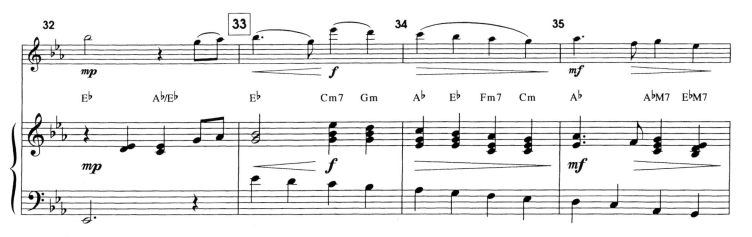

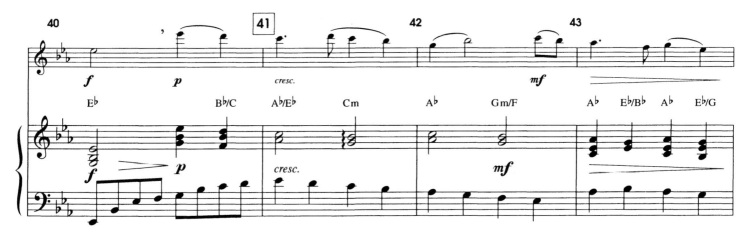

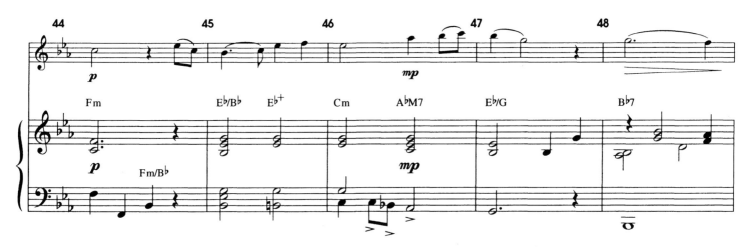

Edvard Grieg
11. ANITRA'S DANCE

Arr. **Ann Lindsay** (ASCAP)

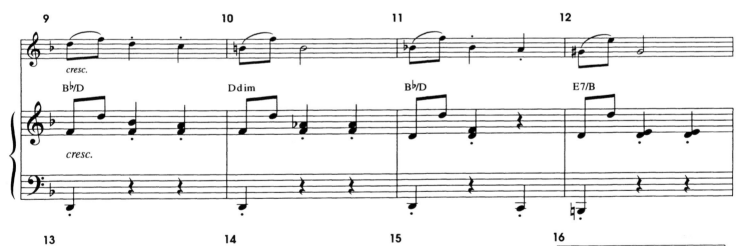

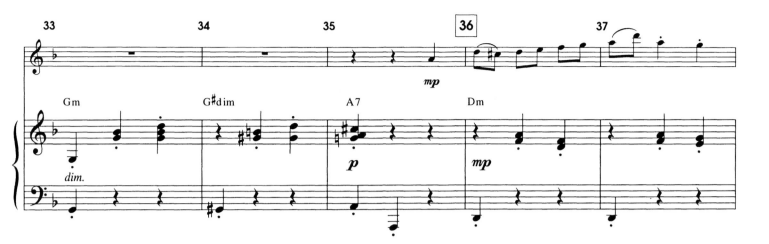

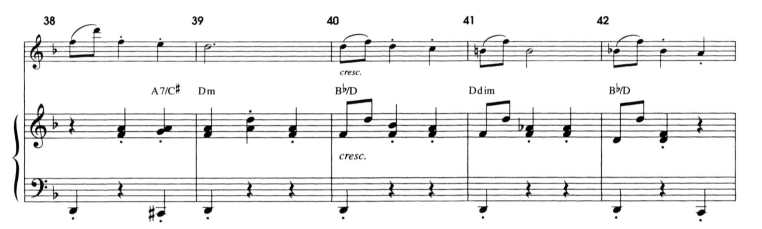

12. AIRE AND DANSE Timothy Johnson (ASCAP)

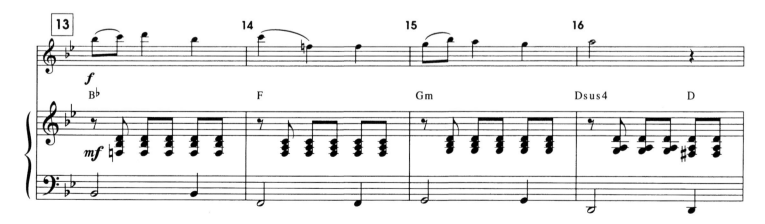

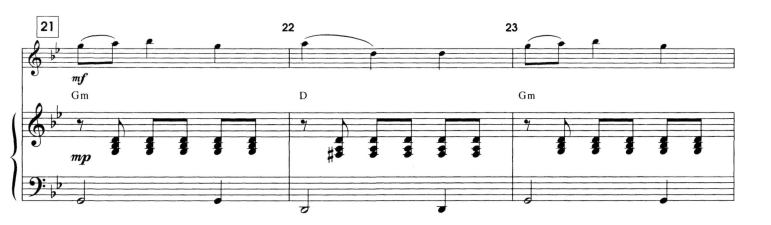

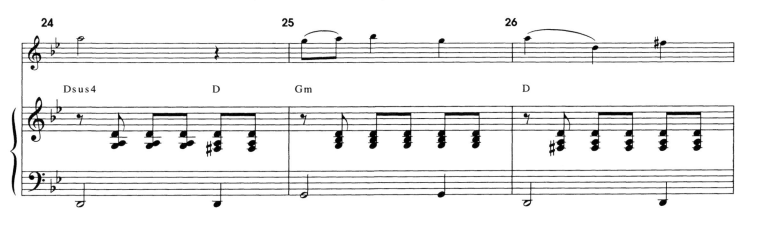

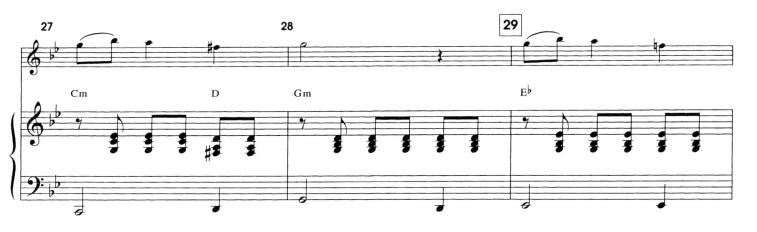

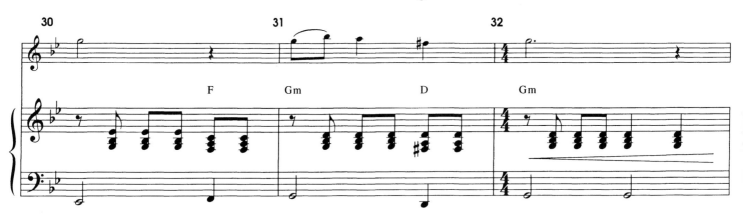

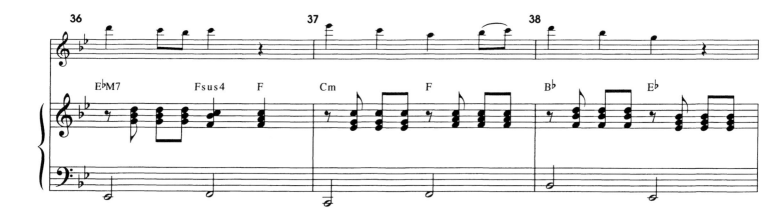

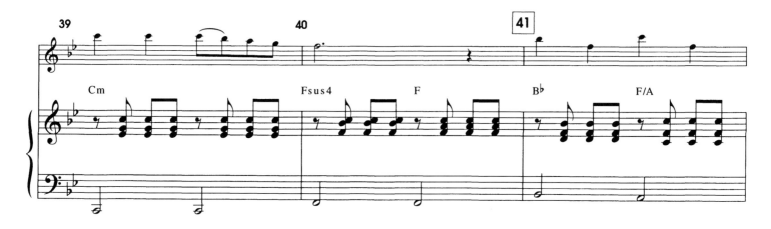

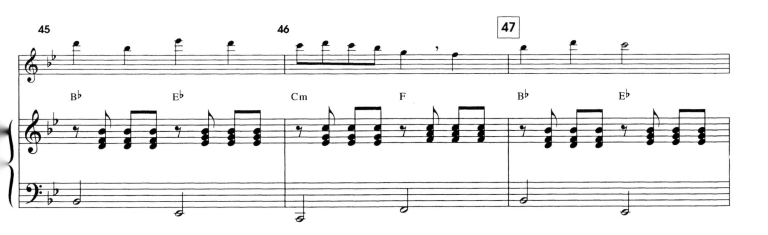

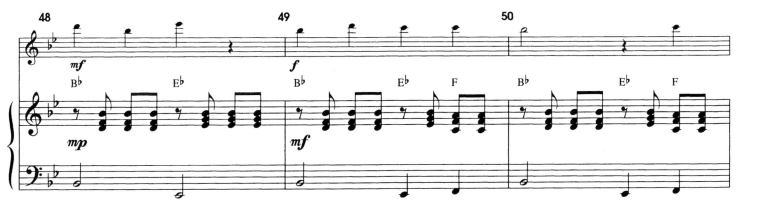

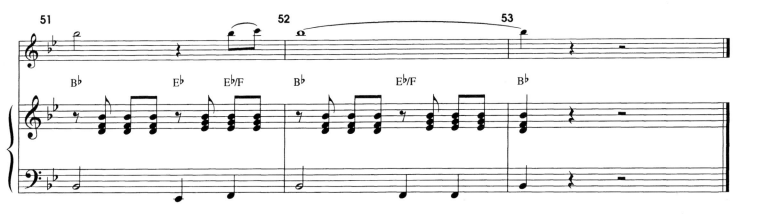